# THE ART OF KITCHEN FITTING – *By Joe Luker.*

## INDEX

# INTRODUCTION

The purpose of this guide is to enable anyone with a reasonable DIY ability to install a kitchen to be proud of.

Using the experience I have gained over the last 35 years, having fitted hundreds of kitchens I will be passing onto you numerous helpful tips, many of which will not be found in other publications.

These tips will save you time and help avoid simple mistakes which are so easily made, especially if this is your first fit.

# GETTING STARTED - TOOLS

Over the years I have accumulated many specialised tools which are necessary if you are fitting professionally but as a one off fit you will get by with the following tools.

NOTE: Tools marked with * are desirable but not essential and can be either hired or in some instances, alternative tools used.

CORDLESS SCREWDRIVER / DRILL

ELECTRIC JIGSAW

1200mm SPIRIT LEVEL

2 X 150mm SPEED CLAMPS (G style)

CLAW HAMMER

CROWBAR / UTILITY BAR * (for ripping out)

SMALL HAND HELD PNEUMATIC HAMMER DRILL 'SDS' (For wall chases and rawlplug fixings)*

2 x TRESTLES (For cutting panels and worktops)*

PLUNGE ROUTER AND WORKTOP JIG * (Necessary for producing professional joints on laminate tops) alternatively use metal jointing strips where tops butt together.

1/2" SHANK STRAIGHT ROUTER CUTTER FOR PLUNGE ROUTER.*

HAND HELD METAL AND VOLTAGE DETECTOR.*

RETRACTABLE TAPE MEASURE.

SET SQUARE

VOLT DETECTOR PEN (a must have tool for testing live cables) SEE BELOW.

HOLLOW ANCHOR SETTING TOOL

 Just touch on outer cable to detect if live

**PLUMBING TOOLS**

15mm AUTOMATIC CIRCULAR PIPE CUTTER

15mm BENDING SPRING

LONG HANDLE PIPE BENDER*

2 X 12" WATERPUMP PLIERS (For 15mm compression fittings and general plumbing)

HEAT MAT

PLUMBERS BLOWTORCH

## CHECK PLAN / DIMENSIONS

If a designer/salesperson has designed your kitchen, you need to double check room dimensions and positions of windows and doors against their provided plan. (They do make mistakes)

**REMEMBER** computer planned does not mean it will fit! The computer is merely a drawing aid and still relies on input from an experienced planner.

**TOP TIP** Always insist on a home visit to allow the designer to either measure the room or check your dimensions.

If your kitchen is ordered on dimensions you have provided you will have the famous "From Customers Own Dimensions" typed on the bottom of your order which means if it doesn't fit TOUGH!

**COMMON PLANNING ERRORS**

1. Kitchen planned too tight

2. Not allowing extra width for free standing appliances i.e. + 30mm for washing machine and +40mm for fridges and freezers.

3. Running waste pipes behind appliances without allowing for extra depth worktops.

4. Siting sockets behind appliances.

5. Not allowing for extra depth worktops on curved or out of true walls (usually older properties)

6. Not allowing extra depth worktops for walls which are not vertical but slant away from the top back edge of the units (usually older properties)

7. Situating appliances on top of mains water inlet pipes (sometimes these can be moved)

8. Placing "L" shaped base and wall units in out of square corners.

9. Not allowing for extra height plinths with badly out of level floors (usually older properties)

10. Placing a worktop cut out for sink or hob adjacent to a corner. Sometimes this cannot this cannot be avoided in very small kitchens.

11. Situating tall housing units in the wrong part of the room making the room appear small.

12. Situating an Island unit in a kitchen which is too small. (These require a large room to look visually acceptable.)

**THESE ARE A FEW PLANNING FAULTS THAT SPRING TO MIND IMMEDIATELY**

# RIPPING OUT – 1st STAGE

**TOP TIP** If the kitchen is in good condition, take photographs whilst it is still in position and advertise it online stating when it will be removed and when it can be collected.

People usually like to view it first before purchasing and it is important that they see the kitchen before it comes out if possible, because it is surprising how a nice kitchen doesn't look quite so nice when the pipe and cable holes are visible.

I myself have purchased many such kitchens for house renovations. NOTE it is usually impractical to re-use old worktops on a new layout.

Used kitchens usually sell easily if you don't go mad on the price and there is the added bonus of not having to make a tip run.

Before commencing any work you need to have a qualified electrician and gas fitter to look over the job so they can be booked in to start work as soon as the kitchen is out.

Ripping out usually takes a day or two to complete.

I usually rip out in the following order:

REMOVE CORNICE PELMETS AND PLINTHS (if present)

REMOVE WALL UNIT DOORS

REMOVE WALL UNIT SHELVES

REMOVE PELMET LIGHTS if present (do undertake this if you are not competent) usually there is a separate switched spur feeding these or they run off the light switch.

REMOVE HOB EXTRACTOR (if present)

**REMOVE WALL UNITS**

Note: units are either visually bolted together or they may be screwed together.

Often these screws are hidden from view behind the hinge back plates which have to be swung down to gain access as in the following illustration.

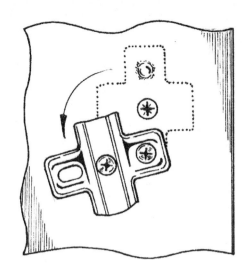

HIDDEN SCREW

## REMOVE BUILT IN OVEN (electric)

First of all switch off the power using the oven isolating switch and double check with the voltage detector stick.

The oven itself will be held in with either two or four small screws which will be visible after opening the oven door (it is amazing how many ovens are just sitting in position without any fixing screws!)

Carefully slide the oven out and place on the floor for disconnection.

If the oven is mounted in a tall housing unit, it is best to slide it out onto a raised work bench or you may find that the cable is too short to lower it down onto the floor (double ovens require two people to lift out due to their awkward shape)

## REMOVE BUILT IN OVEN (gas)

There should be a gas isolating valve in an adjacent base cupboard to allow for disconnection of the oven from the gas supply. This needs to be disconnected by a certified gas fitter who can do any other modifications while he is on site.

Thereafter remove fixing screws as for electric oven.

## REMOVE HOB (electric)

Reach under the worktop and remove any fixing brackets that are retaining the hob in position

Sometimes the hob is held in with silicone making it difficult to remove.

You can try sliding a flat blade between the worktop and the top face of the hob or if that fails, cut into the chipboard laminate worktop with a jigsaw and carefully break away the worktop from the edges of the hob.

## REMOVE HOB (gas)

As per electric hob but gas isolating valve needs to be turned off and hob disconnected from the gas supply by a certified gas fitter who can do any other modifications while he is on site.

# PRELIMARY PLUMBING

### REMOVE SINK

At this stage you need only to disconnect the pipes to the tap(s) and waste pipe from the sink trap.

If there are isolating valves to the tap for hot and cold water simply turn them off and disconnect.

If there are no isolating valves you must turn off the mains cold and hot water by other means.

### COLD SUPPLY

May be just a simple matter of turning off the mains stop cock which could be located in sink base unit or elsewhere in the house. If it cannot be found you will have to turn off the outside mains tap.

While the water is off cut through the 15mm copper pipe which runs up to the tap with a circular pipe cutter and push on a temporary end stop as shown in the diagram below.

The water can now be turned on again.

**NOTE:** Do not cut through the pipe with a hacksaw as this will leave a rough out of square end to the pipe, you need a good square burgh free end to the pipe which the circular cutter will provide. Slide the quick release plastic end stop fully onto the pipe ensuring that it hits the internal stop.

Lubricating the inside of the stop with spittle will allow an easy push fit and for the health conscious, pipes are always flushed out before connecting up to the tap to prevent any possible swarf contamination to the internal tap washers or ceramic disc.

AUTOMATIC CIRCULAR PIPE CUTTER                    PLASTIC END STOP

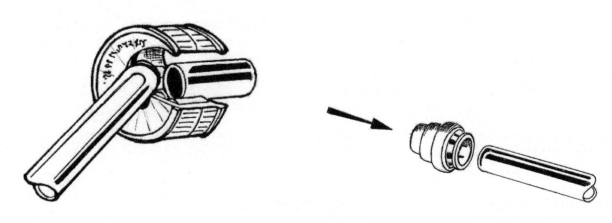

**HOT SUPPLY**   If the house is fitted with a combination boiler, the action of turning off the cold supply to the boiler will also turn off the hot.

Simply test by running the hot tap after the cold is turned off.

If your house has an airing cupboard with a gravity fed heating cylinder you need to stop the water supply from the large water tank in the loft from entering the cylinder.  By doing this the cylinder will no longer be pressurised by the header tank above and hot water will no longer flow from the top exit point of the heating cylinder. (See schematic diagram)

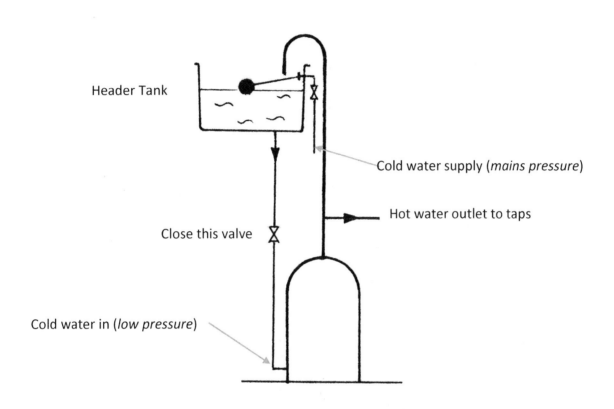

Header Tank

Cold water supply (*mains pressure*)

Hot water outlet to taps

Close this valve

Cold water in (*low pressure*)

## SCHEMATIC OF HOT WATER SUPPLY

There will be an isolating valve in the pipe line from the header tank to the cylinder and this is the valve that needs shutting off.

To check that you have selected the correct valve, simply open the hot water tap at the sink and the flow should stop after allowing a minute or two for the pipe run to drain.

As with the cold supply, push a temporary end stop onto the 15mm copper pipe.

**TOP TIP** Sometimes the valve is seized (especially gate valves) and will not turn off.

If this is the case you can buy a simple rubber conical bung which is twisted into the outlet pipe from inside the header tank thus shutting off the flow without the need to drain down the tank.

**WASTE PIPE**

All that remains now before removing the sink is to disconnect the 40mm plastic waste pipe from the sink waste trap and seal the end of the waste pipe with either tape or a plastic bag with an elastic band. This will prevent foul smells from entering the room.

**REMOVING THE SINK**

The sink is usually secured with metal clips of some kind on the underside and you need to get underneath with a Phillips screwdriver to release them.

In addition to the clips the sink may also be secured with a bead of silicone around the perimeter.

Try breaking the seal with a flat blade and if this fails cut into the worktop with a jigsaw and break away the top around the edges or alternatively if the sink is in a short worktop run, simply remove the top with the sink in it!

**NOTE** there is no need to remove the tap from the sink unless you wish to retain it. (Best to fit new)

**TOP TIP** If there is no other cold drinking water available in the house, fit a temporary stop cock onto the cold pipe that went up to the tap. Position it at a height that you can get a kettle under for making the tea. **"VERY IMPORTANT"**

# RIPPING OUT – 2nd STAGE

**REMOVE DOORS AND SHELVES** from base units and tall housing units if applicable.

**REMOVE ANY REMAINING APPLIANCES** - fridges, microwaves etc., being careful to turn off electricity where applicable. (Check with volt tester)

**REMOVE TILES** from above worktop (if present)

Use either a bolster or wrecking bar of the type shown in the following sketch. I find the wrecking bar is better on plasterboard walls as you can lever the tiles from the wall with less chance of damage.

**SAFETY NOTE :** Removing ceramic tiles can be quite dangerous as a broken tile can be as sharp as a razor blade. Also when levering them from the wall with a flat ended wrecking bar or knocking them off with a club hammer and bolster there is a very high risk of ceramic flakes hitting you in the face or eye.

Picking up the tiles or even just sweeping them off the edge of the worktop into a waste container can cause deep cuts.

For this reason always wear builder's gloves and safety glasses.

**TOP TIP** Sometimes with plasterboard walls it's not possible to remove the tiles without destroying the plasterboard surface in the process. If this happens it's far quicker to remove the damaged plasterboard area and set a new piece in. Take care when removing plasterboard from around sockets, always turn the power off first.

When joining plaster boards always screw a wooden jointing batten behind the butted up panels unless already centralised on a partition stud.

After removing the tiles is usually necessary to give the wall a light skim of plaster to level out any irregularities. This does not have to be a perfect finish as usually it will be retiled or some other surface applied.

**WORKTOP REMOVAL** (Have assumed old tops to be laminated chipboard)

First of all remove all visible screws which are securing the tops down. These are often located on the underside of the base unit front rails but can also screwed through special lugs or brackets.

Worktop joints at corners also have to be separated and can be in the form of simple aluminium strips (often jokingly called salmonella strips in the trade!) which are readily pulled apart or the professional butt and scribe joints which are bolted together on the underside and need loosening with a 10mm spanner.

These bolted joints are usually filled with silicone and part easily by bending the tops up after bolt removal. Sometimes (rarely) they are glued, in which case just jigsaw them apart.

**TOP TIP** Cut any large lengths of worktops into manageable lengths using a jigsaw whilst still on the base units for ease of removal and disposal. (If the tops are siliconed to the wall, use a crowbar to lever them away)

**BASE UNIT REMOVAL**

If the units are not being salvaged the fastest way to remove them is by applying sideward hammer blows to the carcase side panels so that they literally fall apart!

Do not dismantle the sink base unit with all the associated pipework in it for now.

The reason for leaving this unit until last is because this unit needs to be carefully dismantled without damaging the pipework with careless hammer blows and also you need to get the electrics underway by your friendly **QUALIFIED** electrician, so for now just leave the base unit where it is and I will go back to that shortly.

# ELECTRICS

With the room now cleared (apart from the sink base) you can mark on the walls the locations of the base units, the height to the top of the worktops (which is around 910mm in the UK) and also the height to the top and bottom of the wall units. This will aid the electrician for his cable runs and allow you to mark where you would like the sockets to go.

I prefer under worktop appliances to be fed by sockets beneath the tops and simply plugged in through a hole in the base or side wall of the unit. Some people prefer the appliances to run from a switched spur on the back wall above the worktop. I feel this can look messy if you have a lot of them on view (ask your electrician)

Make sure the electrician does not locate any sockets or flex outlet plates behind integrated appliances as these often go right back to the wall with only a few millimetres to spare.

My electrician would always come in at the start and do some preliminary wiring and ask me to give him a ring later for the final connection of appliances and to attach the socket face plates to the boxes after the tiling.

Remember some wiring may have to go behind the wall units to feed extractors, lights etc.

After the electrician has run the cables around the room, installation of the Base Units can commence.

# FIXINGS FOR SECURING BASE AND WALL UNITS TO WALL

**SOLID WALLS:** Use standard plastic wall plugs of a size to accept a 50mm No 4 screw. You will need a suitable masonry drill bit fitted to a hammer drill or preferably an SDS Pneumatic drill which will make light work of the hardest wall.

**WARNING:** Always be aware of possible hidden cables beneath the surface. Use a hand held metal/power detector to check before drilling but remember they will only detect down a small distance. Experience goes a long way in knowing where cables and pipes may be present.

Here are a few clues to look out for:

The chances are that the room skirting board will have been removed along the wall where your base units are positioned. Look carefully at floor level where the wall meets the floor because often the plaster or plasterboard does not quite reach or has broken away and you can often see pipes and cables visible in the small gap left.

Sockets or light switches may have cables rising vertically up or down from them. Remove the faceplate to see which way they go and using a spirit level project up or down to see if they are heading your way.

Below is an example of a little trick that I use quite often.

There is a light switch directly below a back plate which I need to fix to the wall for a wall unit.

The drilling position has been checked with a metal detector and the cable appears to be directly underneath! **DO NOT DRILL AND HOPE YOU WILL MISS!**

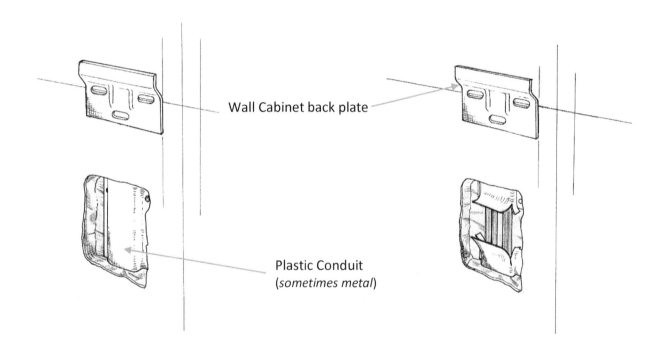

Wall Cabinet back plate

Plastic Conduit
(*sometimes metal*)

**TOP TIP** Below the fixing hole positions, chip out an exploratory hole using a hammer and cold chisel until you expose the cables (turn power off first)

Now you can see exactly where you can drill safely. You may have to drill an additional fixing hole into the back plate to get further away from the cable.

If you need to see exactly where the cables are you can always carefully peel away the conduit if it is the plastic variety. **BE CAREFULL**

PLASTERBOARD WALLS: Metal Hollow Wall Anchors as shown below are in my opinion the best fixings for the job. They fit tightly into the hole and are available in different lengths for various thicknesses of board.

**TOP TIP** Under the flange of the Hollow Wall Anchor which rests against the wall there are two metal spikes which penetrate the plasterboard to prevent any chance of the fixing rotating.

Sometimes I use these fixings to mount heavy objects onto tiled plasterboard surfaces after drilling a suitable hole through the tile using a tile drill.

In this situation you need to squash the metal spikes flat using a pair of pliers to ensure the flange fits nice and square onto the tile.

HOLLOW ANCHOR (Metal)

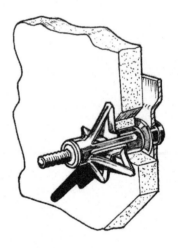

HOLLOW ANCHOR "PULLED UP"

HOLLOW ANCHOR

SETTING TOOL

I came upon these fixings working opposite the Houses of Parliament overlooking the river Thames in London.

The air conditioning lads turned up one day to fix a heavy air conditioning unit onto the plasterboard stud wall that I had erected to create a new kitchen area.

To my amazement they fixed directly to the plasterboard without any internal battens! When I questioned this they gave me a demonstration of how the hollow anchor fixing pulled up with a special tool and explained that providing the plasterboard panels were themselves firmly fixed, the fixings would pull the board off first before failing.

They were right and I have been using them without any problems for the last 30 years!

Up until then I would set wooden battens behind the plasterboard which was very time consuming.

There are other fixings available like the toggle bolt design but these require a hole larger than the bolt diameter which can allow the fixing to drop and also the "Curly Whirly" fixings which are large tapered screw threads with a small screw in the centre which I avoid like the plague as they pull out easily.

**TOP TIP** When drilling into plasterboard walls use a blunt'ish masonry drill bit and hold back the drill with the other hand using it as a stop, so that it does not go firing into the wall at speed. (Do not have the drill set to "hammer") By using a_blunt drill bit you will reduce any possible damage to pipes or cables hidden below the surface when the drill bit breaks gently through.

Sometimes plasterboards are fixed onto a solid wall using the "Dot and Dab" method which is basically dollops of plasterboard adhesive slapped on the back wall at intervals of about 400mm and then the board placed in position and thumped level using a suitable length of heavy wooden batten and a spirit level to check the level as you proceed.

When this method has been used there is a small gap between the solid wall and the underside of the plasterboard which can prevent the Hollow Anchor from going in fully to be pulled up with the tool. To overcome this simply drill through the board as normal but then continue drilling into the back wall to allow the fixing to go home fully so that it can then be pulled up with the tool. SEE BELOW

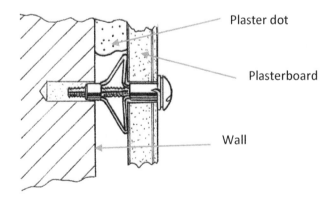

Plaster dot

Plasterboard

Wall

Obviously if you should happen to drill through one of the plaster dots, which will be apparent as there will be no void as you drill through, simple use a standard plastic plug.

# FITTING BASE UNITS

Start with the Corner Base unit. This will either be a single L shaped unit or a single corner base unit. The single base unit has one door, a blanking panel and a corner post, which is either already attached to the unit or in the case of a self- assembly unit, is supplied separately for you to attach as per the makers instructions.

The two types are shown below.

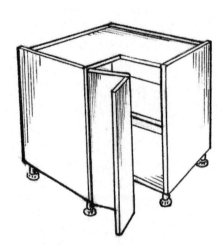

**L Shaped Corner Base**

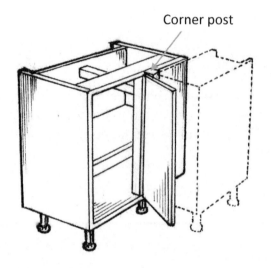

Corner post

**Conventional Corner Base**

Place the base unit into the corner. If the corner is out of square (looking down) the designer should have planned in a conventional corner base unit as obviously the L shaped unit will only fit into a corner which is "near enough square".

## DEALING WITH AN OUT OF SQUARE CORNER (obtuse – over 90°)

The majority of kitchens are usually near enough square to accept either type of corner base unit without any problems.

Out of square corners however are a different story.

The conventional corner base with its separate adjoining unit and corner post can easily cope with the situation but the L shaped unit will not.

If the corner is only slightly out you can sometimes fiddle the L base in by chopping into the plaster.

The only way to successfully overcome the problem with an L shaped corner base in a badly out of square corner is to use an oversize worktop as shown in the following plan view.

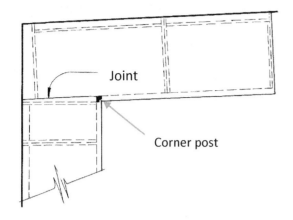

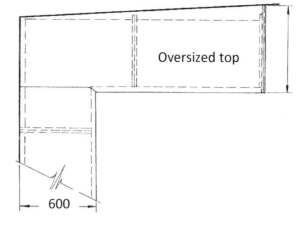

**CONVENTIONAL CORNER BASE**

**L SHAPED CORNER BASE**

### ACUTE CORNER (under 90°)

The same applies with the conventional corner base, again having no problems but this time the oversize top required for the L corner base will be at its widest in the corner rather than the end.

With the unit in position you now need to determine **HOW THE FLOOR RUNS.**

The kitchen will be supplied with plinths which are at a fixed height (usually 150mm, but do vary)

**NOTE:** some kitchens now have **NO** plinths and use the legs as a feature, great for collecting dust underneath but where would we be without fashion!

Assuming your kitchen does in fact have plinths, grab a spirit level (min1200mm) and determine whether the corner in question is at a high or low part of the room in relation to where the other base units are going.

Obviously if you set up your corner base unit to allow a 150mm plinth to fit underneath and the floor dives down at the other end of the room, the standard plinth height will not be high enough at that point. Therefore set the corner base up lower to take this into account.

**TOP TIP** As the units are on adjustable legs I generally set the corner base unit height "near enough" and do a final tweak at the end by lowering or raising the legs on all base units by an equal number of turns.

For this reason although you can screw the units to each other **DO NOT** fix the units to the wall until you are happy with the finished height of all base units.

**TOP TIP** Some base units have an additional centre leg (sometimes two) to prevent cabinet bowing.

An example would be an L shaped corner base or some 1000mm base units.

With these units screw the centre leg(s) up so that it does not touch the floor. Adjust the unit in the normal way until level.

Then place a straight edge on the top of the unit (1200mm spirit level is fine) and unscrew the legs to raise the centre of the unit until it is level with the outer edges.

If you do not do this, the unit tends to swivel on the centre leg(s) and you will be there all day trying to level it.

**IMPORTANT** If the floor is to be tiled, the normal practice is to fit the kitchen first and tile afterwards. Tile up to the front of the base unit legs (not under the units) when the plinths are later fitted they sit on top of the tiles and cover up the rough edge of the tiles.

Wherever you have a free standing appliance which pulls out, remember to tile the full area underneath and back to the wall.

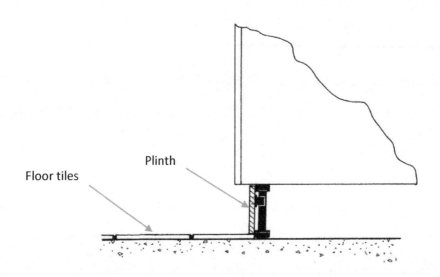

**ELEVATION SHOWING FLOOR TILES AND PLINTH**

IF THE FLOOR IS TO BE TILED AFTER THE FIT, YOU NEED TO SET UP THE BASE UNIT HEIGHTS TO ALLOW FOR THE THICKNESS OF THE TILE AND ADHESIVE IN ADDITION TO THE PLINTH HEIGHT.

If you get into the situation where due to bad floor levels the plastic adjustable legs are wound out and sitting on the last remaining threads, place a wooden packer beneath the foot to get back onto a suitable amount of load bearing thread.

Sometimes customers insist on the complete floor area being tiled and the units placed on top but this is extremely rare.

With the corner base unit in position, levelled and the height set at your best approximation, continue around the room fitting the remaining units.

If the corner base is of the two part type, the **SECOND** unit to be fitted needs to be the one that adjoins it, with the corner post sandwiched in between as per the manufacturer's diagram.

**TOP TIP** When levelling the units, keep them a few millimetres from touching the wall because the back of the unit can drag on the wall and even raise some of the legs off the floor so that you may think that the unit is level but when you pull it away from the wall slightly, it suddenly drops down and you have to start again.

As you place the base units into position you have to keep an eye on what is happening in relation to the wall behind because not all walls rise vertically and can either be leaning in or leaning out.

MOST PROPERTY WALLS ARE NEAR ENOUGH VERTICAL AND POSE NO PROBLEM BUT SOME OLDER STONE WALLED PROPERTIES CAN HAVE WALLS LEANING IN OR OUT WHICH I HAVE COVERED BELOW.

The FIRST DIAGRAM shows the wall at the top leaning into the kitchen which does not really pose any problems and in fact gives you a little more depth under the worktop as you drop down the wall which can be handy for appliances. The one problem it does throw up is the need for a deeper end panel to be scribed into the wall should the base unit not be against an end wall.

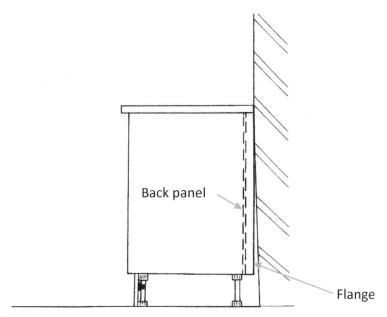

Back panel

Flange

**FIRST DIAGRAM**

However with the wall leaning away from you as in The SECOND DIAGRAM this can throw up a few problems because you will need to modify the unit back flanges to suit the angle of the wall which in turn will reduce the available depth. This in itself is very easy to do using a jigsaw but some integrated appliances (especially dishwashers, fridges and freezers) only have a couple of mm to spare at the rear after they have been pushed back.

I once had a dishwasher that would not go right back because of a cable clip on a 2.5mm power cable running behind was holding it forward!

With such tight tolerances you cannot afford to cut too much from the unit flanges.

Check the actual depth of the appliance to see how much you can safely remove, remembering to allow for the thickness of the cabinet door and fixing bracket on fully integrated appliances.

You can then determine exactly how far the appliance will go back.

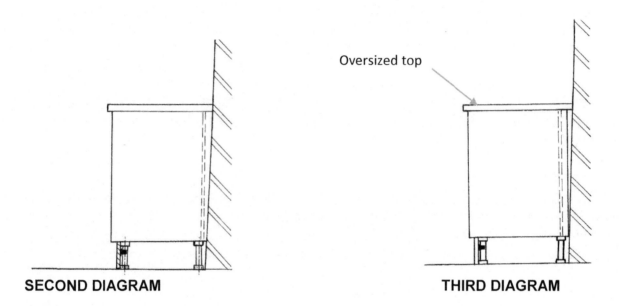

**SECOND DIAGRAM**                                          **THIRD DIAGRAM**

If the wall has a considerable lean to it, the way to overcome the problem is to fit oversize worktops as in the THIRD DIAGRAM or sometimes depending on the wall construction you may gain a few mm by chopping out some of the wall at low level until the appliance fits.

Obviously if there are no appliances in the run you will not require the extra depth tops as long as any drawers which may be present still operate in the reduced depth.

As you work around the room fitting base units you will come to the existing sink base unit which was left in place as mentioned earlier. Now is the time to dismantle the cabinet from around the pipes which may run through it.

Without damaging the pipes, delicately use a saw and hammer to break away the carcase as some of the pipes may run through holes in the base unit

Now you will be left with a collection of pipes from the old layout.

## FITTING THE SINK BASE UNIT

This may be near enough in the same position as before or in a new position.

Either way the 40mm plastic waste pipe needs to enter the new base unit in the correct position either through the back panel of the base unit or up through the unit floor panel. If you are lucky it may be just be a case of shortening or lengthening the existing pipe and if the pipe goes through the wall to an outside gully you may even be able to still use the same exit hole.

If you are unlucky a new hole may be required through the wall and even two holes as it is quiet common to have one hole for the sink and another for the washing machine waste which may be situated away from the sink

If the existing waste pipe is cemented into the floor then again you must somehow get back onto this. If the designer has planned an appliance on top of the cemented waste pipe (Let's hope not!!) chop the floor out and bury the pipe.

**TOP TIP** Over the years I have found it far easier to clear out the old pipework from under the sink and start again because it is rarely in the correct position and usually in a mess.

Below is a sketch of what you need to end up with the new sink base in position.

The hot and cold pipes enter at the rear of the base and come up through the floor of the unit just in front of the back panel. (These pipes do not have to be directly in line with the tap above and I intentionally offset them to allow for a nice sweeping curve from the flexible hose to the tap) The unit is then lowered over the pipes after drilling two holes in the correct position and of a large enough diameter to pass over the plastic end stops. Once the unit is in place and levelled against the others fit valves of your choice onto the two pipes. Traditionally this would be a 15mm stop cock on the cold and a 15mm gate valve on the hot but now I often use <u>full bore</u> lever valves) do not use the small ballofix type valves with the screwdriver slot in them as they can be difficult to shut off in a hurry and more importantly they greatly reduce the flow rate due to their small internal bore which can have a big effect on the hot flow if it is gravity fed.(Note this type of valve is also available "large bore" but would still not recommend a screwdriver slot turn off, on a main shut off valve. **SEE ALSO UNDERSINK PLUMBING** (Final connections)

Keep the two valves as low as possible as this will provide plenty of room above the valves to tee off to the dishwasher, washing machine etc. (The final connections to the taps etc. will take place after the tops are in and sink in position.)

### REMEMBER HOT ON THE LEFT - COLD ON THE RIGHT

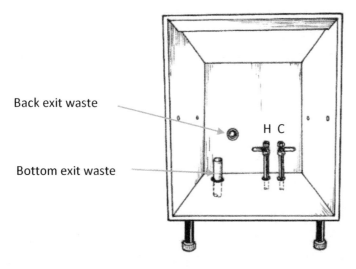

Back exit waste

Bottom exit waste

H C

## HOW TO FIX THE BASE UNITS TO THE WALL

Fixings vary with the make of the units. Some base units have a back rail flush with the wall (worst type as difficult to modify for out of true walls) which you drill through into the wall behind.

Others (If they are rigid built) sometimes have small angle brackets already fixed to them to accept suitable screws.

Other makes have no fixing points or brackets at all and you place your own metal angle brackets onto the void flanges at the rear in positions to suit yourself.

AS MENTIONED EARLIER DO NOT FIX BASE UNITS BACK TO THE WALL UNTIL YOU ARE HAPPY WITH THE PLINTH CLEARANCE UNDERNEATH THE UNITS. THIS SHOULD ACCEPT THE FULL HEIGHT PLINTH AT THE LOWEST POINT OF THE FLOOR AND THE PLINTH IS THEN TAPERED AS THE FLOOR RISES.

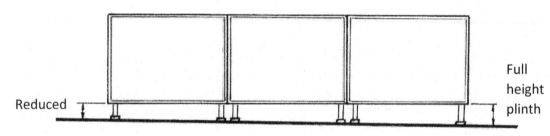

Reduced                                          Full height plinth

**UNEVEN FLOOR** ( exaggerated)

## SCREWING THE UNITS TO EACH OTHER

There are special bolts for screwing units together and when I first started out I did use them, however all fitters that I know do not use these bolts for the following reasons.

They are visible

They are time consuming to fit

They cost more and have no advantage over a conventional screw

You could argue that screws do not have the holding power of a bolt but providing the units are levelled up correctly and fit snuggly together without straining to pull them together (which should never be the case) a screw is perfectly adequate as units are not subjected to sideward forces.

The following sketch shows how I fix the base and wall units together. Two 150mm speed clamps are essential to make a good job of this.

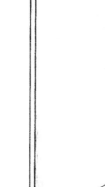

## FIXING UNITS TOGETHER (Wall and Base)

With both units level, clamp the two front edges of the units together as shown in the drawing.

Now remove the top screw from the hinge back plate and slightly loosen the bottom screw so that the back plate swings down as shown in the next diagram.

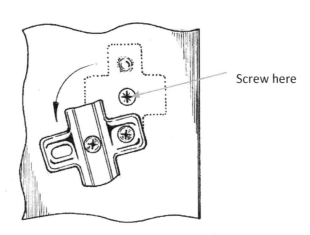

Screw here

Use a screw length which is under the thickness of the two panels. So for 18mm carcases use a 30mm screw. (Do not go any less as you need enough to bite into the second panel)

Using a cordless screwdriver insert a screw roughly between the two back plate fixing holes.

Repeat for the other hinge and then swing the plates back up and lightly secure thus concealing the cabinet fixing screws.

You can fix a couple more screws towards the rear of the cabinet if you feel it needs it.

# COMMON PROBLEMS ENCOUNTERED FITTING BASE UNITS

Often there are obstructions that prevent the base units from going in.

Pipework can often be moved but you may have something that needs to stay put like a soil pipe or a section of wall that steps out.

In these instances the base unit will need to be modified by reducing its depth. This is fairly easy with a self-assembly unit but if it has a working drawer this may have to be sacrificed with a dummy drawer front.

For rigid units (supplied assembled and glued) you can sometimes get away with sawing the complete carcase to its new depth and fixing the back panel back on with battens or you may have to very carefully knock it apart which can be tricky and involve inserting hacksaw blades between the panels to saw through the dowels. (Choose the best option for the situation)

Some of the better companies will give you the option to order a base unit in a "dry" form (unglued) which makes modification easy.

In some circumstances you may be lucky and only have to move the back panel forward and leave the unit full depth.

Sometimes you may have to reposition one of the legs and again you may have to resort to the faithful hacksaw blade to cut through some of the expanding drive pin type of leg fixings.

 (Don't be tempted to knock em out with a big "ammer" it will take part of the floor panel with it)

# WORKTOP SUPPORT PANELS

Sometimes you may have two **free standing** appliances side by side, say a fridge and a freezer and these will require a worktop support panel between them.

The front edge of worktop support panel should be level with the front edge of the **DOORS** on adjacent units **NOT** the carcase. If by doing this it creates a gap between the back of the panel and the wall this does not matter.

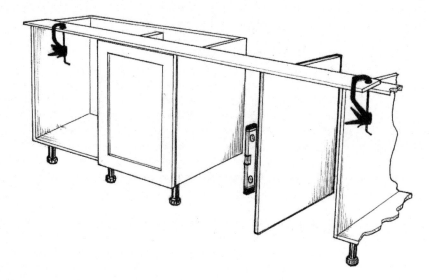

**ALINEMENT TRICK USING PLINTH**  (See following TOP TIP)

**TOP TIP** To obtain the exact front edge of the worktop support panel, clamp a piece of the kitchen plinth onto the top front rails of fitted base units as shown above level with the front of the cabinet <u>door</u>. (Temporarily fit a cabinet door to achieve this)

Even where there are no support panels I always clamp a length of plinth onto the units as it provides a visual means of monitoring how the base run is progressing .Some walls are not straight but by continually checking the dimension from the back of the wall to the front of the plinth you can make any adjustments to the units as you progress (some units may end up being away from the wall slightly and others may need a touch taken off the back flanges to keep the line going.)

**NOTE** it is not necessary to fix every base unit to the wall as the base run will become "as one" and will only need fixing at intervals (The worktop fixings screws will also tie the units together.)

## PROCEDURE FOR FITTING THE WORKTOP SUPPORT PANEL.

Determine panel position by marking back wall (for FREE STANDING appliances there must be a side clearance to allow for either movement or ventilation)

SUGGEST Washing machine + 30/40mm, fridge or freezer + 40mm (ALWAYS CHECK

MANUFACTURERS RECOMMENDATION)

With the panel siting loosely in position check that the front edge is vertical. If not hold it in a vertical position to determine how much needs to come off the bottom by scribing a line on the panel to take into account an out of level floor.

Cut the bottom of the panel and recheck.

Again holding the panel loosely in position, mark the top of the panel to align with the top of adjacent base units and cut to final length (support panels are usually supplied extra length to allow for cutting in)

If all is well you can now secure the panel to the floor and wall using suitably sized metal angle brackets.

# BASE END PANELS

Base end panels are used to tidy up the ends of unit runs and give a more pleasing look as the panels go to the floor and there is no need to return plinths around the end.

They can also be used in the middle of a run, for instance either side of a slot in cooker as shown in the next diagram. This means that you can just butt the plinths up to the panels which is much easier and looks more professional.

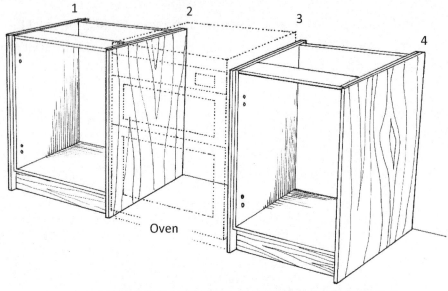

**USE OF BASE END SUPPORT PANELS X 4**

# INTEGRATED APPLIANCES

For an integrated appliance you just leave a space between two units for it to slot in. If on the end of a run the space will be between a unit and a base end panel.

The space will be the same as the appliance width going in. So for a 600 dishwasher leave a 600mm gap, a 450mm dishwasher a 450mm gap, 600 fridge a 600mm gap. The appliance is usually slightly smaller in size, for example 595, 445 etc.

**TOP TIP** Make up three simple spacer bars as shown below. Place between the gap and leave them in position until all of the base units are fixed in.

These will ensure that the aperture stays at the correct width for the appliance to slide in later.

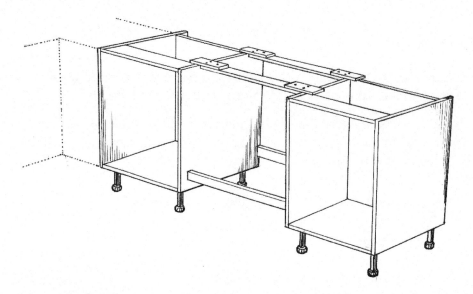

**TEMPORARY SPACER BARS**

If you have two **integrated** appliances side by side like a fridge and freezer, do not fit a worktop support panel in between them because when you fit the cabinet doors the visible panel in between will spoil the run.

As a support panel is not present, I raise the appliances up on the adjustable legs until they are flush with the tops or the cabinets.

Unfortunately some of the adjustable legs on integrated appliances are a bit on the flimsy side when they are wound out and if the machine has to be pulled out for repairs, the legs can sometimes snap off! For this reason I often raise the legs on wooden battens screwed to the floor so that the legs are well into their threads for maximum stability and less likely to snap off when the appliance is pulled out.

If you do this, be sure not to use chipboard worktop off cuts for battens. I did this once on a big job in Central London many years ago and a flood then occurred on the ground floor (not my doing)

This resulted in the chipboard battens vastly increasing in thickness due to water absorption and subsequently pushing the base units up through the worktops and cracking the tiles as well (you live and learn)

Some appliance manufactures have only 3 legs on their machines and these are GREAT as levelling is "a piece of cake" simply slide in, adjust the central back leg from the front of appliance using the screw rod and then level the two front legs manually. (If you batten up the three legged variety all three battens need to run full length from front to back like the four leggers)

## FITTING AN INTEGRATED OR FREESTANDING DISHWASHER / WASHING MACHINE

Before sliding the appliance into position you need to study the rear pipework layout carefully.

Nowadays there is only a cold water feed hose to a washing machine, having dispensed with the hot fill. The machine does all the heating now which was always the case really if you think about it because when the hot water was drawn it would usually run cold for some time.

You need to decide where to drill holes into the side of the sink base unit to run the fill and waste hoses and also the power cable.

On a washing machine the flexible waste hose comes from the bottom and the fill pipe usually enters at the top. The fill pipe is usually held onto the machine with a hand tightened plastic flange nut which can be loosened to allow the right angled connection to be rotated to either a horizontal or vertical position to suit the application.

The two rear sides, top and bottom of the machine normally have a recess for the hose to run in so that the machine can go back to the wall.

Dishwashers also have the waste coming from the bottom but the fill can be top or bottom.

Below shows a typical hose arrangement for a washing machine and dishwasher

**NOTE:** Washing machine standpipe waste could be in an adjacent cupboard depending on the location of the machine.

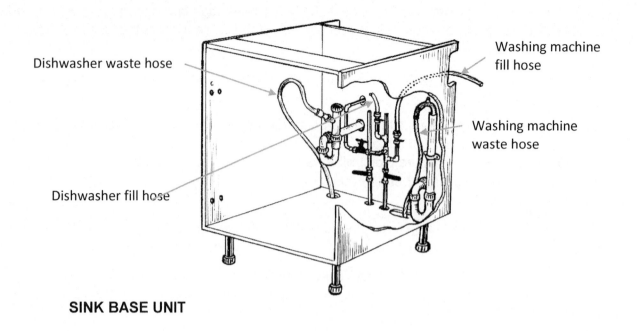

Dishwasher waste hose

Washing machine fill hose

Washing machine waste hose

Dishwasher fill hose

**SINK BASE UNIT**

**TOP TIP** The waste hose from the dishwasher can connect to a sink spigot waste trap but you must remember to tie up hose as high as possible just below the level of the drainer with a cable clip to prevent back syphoning and leave dirty water in your dishwasher.

With the washing machine I always run the waste into a separate standpipe waste fitting.

Years ago I would simply connect the washing machine waste hose into the spigot trap alongside the dishwasher but started receiving complaints of soap suds coming up through the plug hole!

**INTEGRATED FRIDGE AND FREEZERS**

These are relatively easy having just a power cable.

Raise the machines up to the underside of the worktop (wooden battens if necessary) as mentioned previously.

Drill a large enough hole through the cabinet to allow for the power plug using a hole cutter.

Remember to follow the manufacturer's instructions as these appliances usually have trims and cover strips in abundance.

**TOP TIP** Fit all integrated appliances before the worktops go on as it is far easier to feed them in and level them.

Without the tops on you can keep an eye on the pipes and cable at the rear by tilting the machine as it pushes in.

Also try to keep L shaped fixing brackets used to hold the worktops down, out of the appliance aperture as they can catch on the side of the appliance and prevent it going in smoothly.

**\* DO NOT FIT WORKTOPS AT THIS STAGE \***

# FITTING WALL UNITS

These are fitted after the bases because sometimes there are problems with out of square corners etc. which means that the base units may be a few mm out of their designated positions.

With the base units already in, you can now project a line up with a spirit level to ensure that the wall cupboards are in alinement.

## SETTING THE HEIGHT

The manufacturers will have a height that they recommend their units to be set at which you should follow.

If there is a tall appliance housing or larder unit in the plan this would have been fitted with the base units and this will automatically determine the height to the top of the wall units.

If there is one present, the first wall unit that you fit should be the one that attaches to it.

## SETTING THE ADJUSTABLE WALL HANGER

Most wall units these days are fitted with fully adjustable wall brackets which is what I will deal with here.

There are many types of hangers used but they all have a back plate which fixes to the wall and an adjustable hanger which fixes to the cabinet.

Each wall hanger is equipped with adjustable screws for "up and down" as well as "in and out" positioning

Place the wall unit onto a work bench or similar and wind the adjustable hanger to its mid position so that when it is attached to the fixed wall bracket you will have the option to raise or lower the cabinet in either direction.

Having set the adjuster to midway position, hold a back plate under the wall hanger at the rear of the cabinet and measure down from the top of the unit to either the top of the back plate or the hole centres in the bracket and use this dimension to project around the room as a datum line for the other back plates.

## FIXING THE BACK PLATES TO THE WALL

You can mark all of the wall cabinet positions onto the wall and then come back inside the vertical lines and mark where the edge of the back plate will be. For instance if the cabinets are 18mm thick, mark back 20mm to make sure that the plates will fit comfortable between the unit side flanges. You can then fix all of the back plates in one go and then loosely hang all of the units before starting back at the first one which can then be pulled back to the wall and levelled up with the relevant screws (but not too tight at this stage)

Accuracy is extremely important when marking out the back plate positions.

If you decide to mark the wall out for all of the brackets in one go, be sure to make all dimensions from the first datum line, ie for three 1000mm wall units you need to measure 1000mm, then 2000mm, then 3000mm to avoid an accumulation of errors.

Alternatively you could move along fitting and marking one cabinet at a time.

**TOP TIP** When levelling the wall units be aware that the level can alter as the unit is pulled back tight to the wall from the hanging forward position.

Always recheck the cabinet as it is pulled back tight against the wall using the in/out adjustment.

### SCREWING THE WALL UNITS TO EACH OTHER

Screwing the units together is the same as described for the base units using the clamps and hiding the screws under the hinge back plates. If there are no back plates to conceal the screws place them neatly the same distance in from the front edge (approx. 25mm)

NOTE some countersunk screws now have serrated ribs on the underside of the countersink to aid pulling into timber as they act like miniature cutters. Best to avoid these when fixing into decorative laminate boards such as kitchen cabinets because they chip out the laminate and look unsightly.

As you progress around the room fitting your wall cabinets keep an eye on the underside of the units to make sure that they are still butted up tight to each other where they touch the wall. If the wall is not straight they can start to concertina apart as they try and follow the wall profile.

If this starts to happen, release some of the hanger screws which pull the units back to the wall and allow the gap to close.

Sometimes I add a few joining screws at the rear of the cupboard if necessary (you can hide them behind the shelves)

# HOB EXTRACTOR – DUCT TO OUTSIDE ( If applicable )

If you have an extractor which requires ducting through an outside wall then you need to drill a large diameter hole to accept the flexible or rigid ducting.

Ducting sizes vary but most are either 100mm or 150mm in diameter.

There are two ways to drill the hole.

**METHOD ONE:** Preferably using an SDS electric drill, bore a hole through the wall in the centre of the proposed ducting location. (The drill bit needs to be long enough to pass through the wall in one hit and of approximately 16mm in diameter) Then drill a series of holes around this centre hole but only half way through if a solid wall or just through the first the first layer if a cavity. Then go to the outside and drill from the other direction.

Now using a hammer and cold chisel or an SDS electric drill set in chisel mode (if it has one) with the appropriate chisel bit, you can break away the pieces between the series of holes to remove the two plugs.

**TOP TIP** If the new ducting hole is within a few inches of an existing hole from the previous layout you can leave the exit hole on the outside wall where it is which means no remedial work on the outside wall.

To achieve this just drill at a slight angle towards the exit hole and use flexible ducting.

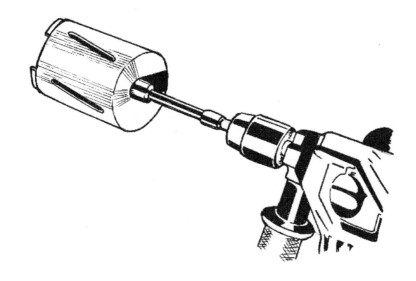

**DIAMOND CORE DRILL**

**METHOD TWO:** Use a Diamond Core Bit of the correct diameter.

These will pass through the wall fairly easily but are extremely expensive and also require a decent electric drill with lowdown torque, although I have used the SDS electric drill successfully with the hammer function OFF. (Prime candidate for the hire shop)

## TYPES OF WORKTOPS

Laminated Chipboard

Granite

Solid wood

Corian

Other materials are also used such as slate, marble and tiled tops but not so much.

**LAMINATED CHIPBOARD** Available in various thicknesses and was until fairly recently the most popular form of work surface but more and more people are now going over to Granite.

Laminate surfaces can be fitted by DIY enthusiasts with either simple butted joints using aluminum jointing strips or by the more specialised system using a Butt and Scribed joint together with three worktop jointing bolts which can only be performed successfully by using a router and worktop jig.

For this reason you may wish to leave this part of the fit to a professional kitchen fitter or hire the very expensive "heavy duty" router and jig to undertake the work.

**SPECIAL NOTE**: High Gloss Laminate Tops require special mention because they are very easily scratched despite what the salesman said!

When making any cuts always apply masking tape to the decorative surface so that you can see the pencil line and also prevent the base plate of any saw marking the surface.

Also be sure to place cloths over any trestles to prevent damage.

High gloss tops have lost me more time and money than anything else due to tops being scratched on delivery and having to wait for replacements which have also been scratched!

**GRANITE** After fitting the kitchen you invite a granite supplier to come in and make the actual size templates for your tops.

The templates are made using thin MDF or plastic corrugated sheets which are then taken away to produce your tops after which they return and fit them. (They would already have given you a price from the initial plan drawing)

**CONSIDERATIONS TO TAKE INTO ACCOUNT WITH GRANITE.**

Granite is extremely heavy and base units may need beefing up in places as you feel fit.

The base unit plastic legs will take the weight alright providing they have plenty of threads engaged. Base units and especially any support panels need to extremely level as unlike chipboard tops, granite does not like to be flexed too much.

The main kitchen floor should be solid with no flexing.

Concrete floors are obviously fine or concrete covered with rigid insulation and chipboard is also acceptable but suspended joists with chipboard or floorboards can cause problems and may not be suitable.

Problems with suspended joists consist of the floor dropping over time and leaving a gap between the worktops and the tiling as well as levels going out of true.

Worst still the joists may have woodworm or rot!

I once fitted a granite topped kitchen onto a floorboard floor which although "sound" was flexing before I even started! Fortunately there was a 600mm void under the floor and I was able to get underneath and support the joists with large timber props. By the time I was done it looked like the mine scene from "Indiana Jones".

Granite tops are secured to the base units with silicone.

Often with granite tops special stainless steel under mount sinks are used and set beneath the granite. With these you will need a separate plywood base board which fits between the full top area of the sink base unit and has a hole cut in it for the sink to drop into.

The board should be set below the top level of the unit so that when the sink is dropped in there is a gap of approximately 1mm between the top face of the sink and the underside of the granite top to allow for a seam of clear silicone.

The easiest way to fix the precise positioning of the board is to simply screw through the sides of the cabinet straight into the board with additional supporting brackets under, if you feel fit.

**SOLID WOOD** Usually Oak but other timbers available.

As with laminated chipboard, well within the scope of DIY.

Can be simply butted together at the joint due to the square section of the Worktop which does not require the worktop router jig to produce the 45° start angle which is required on the rounded edge profile of a laminate top.

Bolt together with 3 bolts using the router jig for the bolt slots and silicone in the joint.

Once fitted, these tops are given several coats of Danish Oil (sanding between) which needs to be repeated every year or two depending on use.

**CORIAN** Brand name for a material manufactured from acrylic polymer and alumina trihydrate which is derived from bauxite ore.

Corian has the advantage of seamless joints which means that a worktop could be fitted with a hole left in it for the sink and then a Corian sink bowl could dropped in and clamped together with a two part epoxy resin. The end result is a sink that is "as one" with the worktop with no detectable seams.

The material is warm to touch and available in many colours and surface effects. It can be repaired and surface scratches removed by buffing.

**DISADVANTAGES** more expensive than even Granite and must be fitted by a "Du Pont" certified fabricator. (He will make templates on his first visit)

## CUTTING AND JOINTING WORKTOPS (Laminated chipboard and Wood)

The following sketch of a typical corner arrangement shows the sink positioned close to the corner and the worktop joint is located away from the sink bowl.

The reason for this is to keep the joint away from the sink cut out and reduce the risk of water penetrating and "blowing" the top if it is laminated chipboard. Also if the joint is a butt and scribe bolted assembly, the sink cut is out away from the bolts.

**TOP TIP** Never allow water to remain pooled over a worktop joint as blowing can occur if water enters the joint.

Always wipe off.

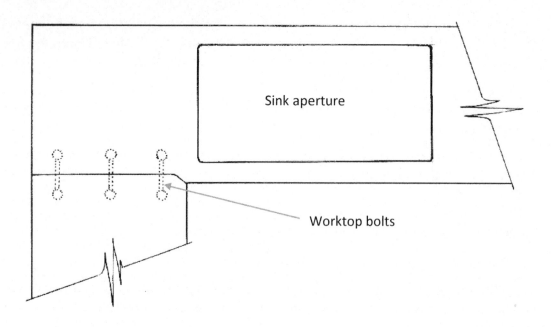

Sink aperture

Worktop bolts

**WORKTOP PLAN VIEW**

**PLEASE NOTE:**

WITH CHIPBOARD LAMINATED WORKTOPS YOU COULD AS AN ALTERNATIVE SIMPLY USE AN ALUMINIUM JOINTING STRIP AT THE JOINT AND ALSO AN ALUMINIUM END STRIP ON THE END OF THE WORKTOP.

SOLID WOOD TOPS WITH THEIR SQUARE PROFILES CAN BE BUTTED DIRECTLY AND BOLTED AS PER THE CHIPBOARD LAMINATE.

**1) POSITION THE "SINK RUN" TOP ONTO THE BASE UNITS AND PUSH HARD UP TO THE CORNER**

The length of the top should be approx. 70mm longer than the finished length to allow for scribing in and finishing off the end.

Check how the end of the board fits against the wall. It does not have to be a perfect fit because the tiles will cover up any small gaps.

If there is a tapered gap due to an angled corner you need to scribe a line onto the top using a spacer block as shown and cut the top accordingly. It helps to apply some masking tape to see the pencil line more easily, especially on black or gloss tops.

Again the saw cut does not have to be chip free as the tiles will cover.

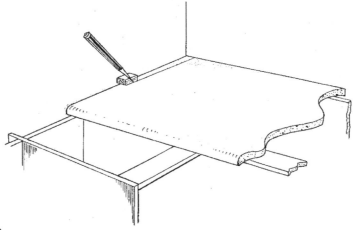

## SCRIBING IN WORKTOP

CUTTING WORKTOP JOINTS WITH A ROUTER AND JIG IS PROBABLY THE HARDEST PART OF THE FIT AND WOULD ADVISE STRONGLY AGAINST TRYING THIS YOUSELF UNLESS YOU ARE COMPETENT.

(Find a kitchen fitter who will undertake this for you if need be)

**TOP TIP** When using a plunge router on worktops make the first plunge run at approximately 2mm / 3mm depth to penetrate through the hard laminate surface and then go down in increments of about 6mm to make life easy and prevent heat build up which reduces cutter life.

## 2) CUT THE FEMALE WORKTOP JOINT "SINK RUN"

With the worktop resting on trestles cut the female joint first before the male using the worktop jig and router.

I am not going to explain this in great detail as there are different types of jigs available, though most have locating pins to ensure correct location and clamps to secure onto the top.

If this is your first time using a router I would strongly recommend that you practice on an off cut before plunging into an expensive worktop and follow the jig makers instructions. You will find practical demonstrations on "You Tube".

### Here are some tips to help you:

As you will see, the two joint starts with a 45° angle which is necessary to allow two rounded profile boards to meet. It is important that you cut "into" the joint with the cutter. If the cutter exits the 45° angle you will get chipping and tearing out of the laminate.

To prevent this you may have to turn the board over and cut on the reverse side so that the cutter starts by cutting into the angle. (Hope that makes sense)

**NOTE:** On some of the worktop jigs available you can make an opposite hand cut without turning the board over but the one I have is not reversible. Just remember to always cut into the 45° angle and you will not go wrong.

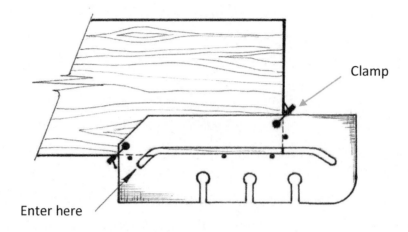

Clamp

Enter here

CUTTING FEMALE JOINT

## WORKTOP ROUTER JIG

After you have cut the first joint fit the worktop back onto the base units in its correct location but this time prop it up from the work top using battens of timber the same thickness as the top (Worktop off cuts are perfect)

Now place the hob run top onto the base units on the other wall and slide it carefully up to the female joint and just as it is about to touch, lift up the sink run top to allow it to slide gently under by approx. 50mm.

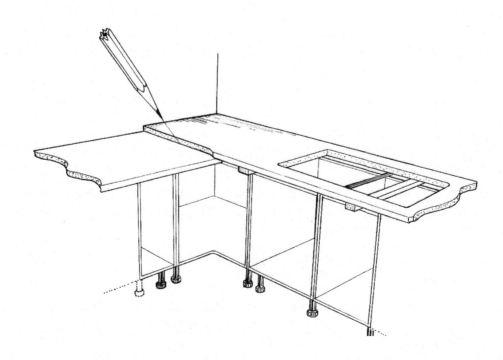

**TOP TIP** Sliding the top underneath the takes into account the possibility of the corner not being at 90°. It is permissible to cut out of angle for a few degrees using the jig but for severely out of true corners you must revert to dissecting the angle in half with two straight edge cuts.

Now mark the bottom worktop with a pencil (preferably with masking tape applied to see the line) and remove worktop and place on trestles for cutting the male joint.

### 3) CUT MALE WORKTOP JOINT "HOB RUN"

When cutting the male joint I find it easier to set up the jig so that the cutter is only cutting through half of its diameter as this reduces the cutting time and prolongs cutter life.

### 4) CUT THE JOINTING BOLT SLOTS

I personally fit three 150mm bolts per joint and do not use biscuit joints.

Some fitters do use the "biscuits" but I find that they can prevent the joint from being nice and flush when you finally hammer them into position.

The slot positions that I use are shown below for a standard 600mm depth top but these positions can be varied.

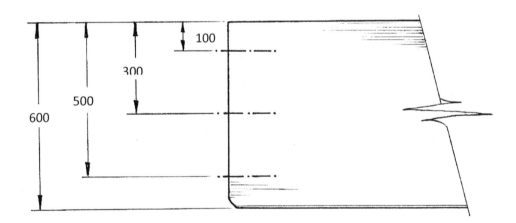

On a 40mm thickness top I usually plunge down about 20/25 mm which is set on the router depth stop.

After making the first plunge I then go around the outer edge of guide making a series of plunges and then join them all up at the end by running the router in one continuous sweep.

### 5) CUT BOARD TO FINISHED LENGTH

With the work top in position and sink hole cut you will have an overhang at the end of the run.

Mark the underside of the top with a pencil where the last unit ends and cut off the surplus after leaving another 5mm or so for overhang.

If the end is to accept a laminate strip the cut should be performed with a router fitted with the same 1/2" straight fluted router cutter as used on the joints to give a chip free end, otherwise just apply an aluminium end strip which will cover up any small saw chips.

**TOP TIP** When cutting laminate surfaces with a jigsaw you can buy what are commonly known as upside down blades which cut on the downward stroke and do not cause chipping.

Use with care as they try and push the saw upwards so apply a downward pressure and do not use "pendulum cut" if available on your jigsaw.

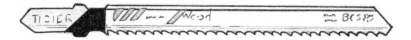

For worktops I use a conventional jigsaw blade (usually "plunge cut") as slight chipping does not matter but on thinner cabinet boards which require a "show" edge I use the reverse cut blade above.

## WORKTOP CUTOUTS FOR SINK HOB ETC

With the worktop in position and the sink placed upside down on the worktop, carefully locate it into its correct position ensuring that the bowl(s) will be contained within the cabinet below.

Then slide some masking tape face down, halfway under the edges of the sink perimeter and press down

After re-checking the position mark around the entire sink outline with a pencil.

Now refer to the sink manufacturer's instructions which usually tell you to mark inside of the line you have just drawn by 10mm and this will be your cutting line.

To cut out the sink hole first drill a hole large enough to accept the jigsaw blade and cut around the inner pencil line.

**TOP TIP** You can dispense with the drill hole and plunge the jigsaw straight in with the following method. (You will need an 'ADVANCED PLUNGE CUT BLADE')

Hold the jigsaw well away from the edge towards the centre (in case it jumps and marks the top) and simply tip the saw up as shown by pivoting on the front of the base plate and lower. Do this slowly and make sure that 'pendulum cut' is 'off' if your jigsaw has this feature, otherwise the saw may start jumping across the worktop wreaking havoc as it goes.

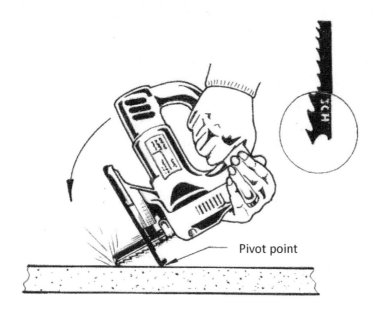

Pivot point

If there are other holes to be cut such as the HOB this should be done now.

## WORKTOP CORNER JOINT

If the joint is located above a 900 L shaped corner base you need to mark on the top panel or top rails of the unit where the 3 bolts will be sited.

The bolting up is performed lying on your back inside the unit with the worktops in their final position.

(Any internal unit shelves should be lowered down to the base panel with support pegs removed)

Where you have marked the bolt positions on top of the unit, remove areas with a jigsaw to provide spanner access from underneath. See below.

Cut out for bolts

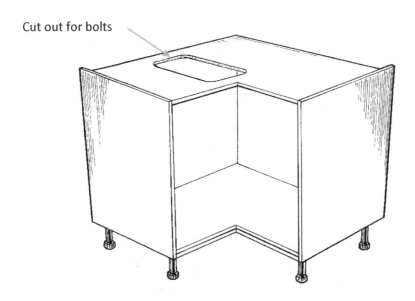

Now get everything ready and close at hand for the "bolt up" as you need to keep going once started.

**You Will Need:** 3 Worktop jointing bolts, Small club hammer, 100mm square "off cut" from unit carcase (For whacking), 10mm open ended spanner, clear silicone or coloured to suit, metal blade(to remove surplus silicone) cloth (for final cleaning up), crowbar (sometimes required for compressing up joints)

Apply silicone to one half and push the two edges together, then get underneath with the bolts ready for insertion. (I lay the two bolts on my chest ready for insertion.)

Take one of the bolts and adjust the length so that it just fits into the span with a slight push, then with one finger supporting the centre of the bolt start tightening the nut but not too much just enough to pull up the joint slightly.

Now repeat with the other bolts but be sure to keep an eye on 45° angle at the front of the joint and make sure it is tight up. If it needs tightening up, the easiest way is use a crow bar or even a wood chisel between the wall and the worktop to lever the joint up.

As you continue to evenly tighten the bolts, keep removing the surplus "squeeze out" from above the joint using flat metal blade like the end of a metal rule.

Using the block of wood and the club hammer, apply blows to the top laminate face of the worktop either side of the joint to bring the two surfaces flush and then tighten some more.

Keep tightening and leveling up with the hammer until you are satisfied with the joint and the bolts are starting to get hard to turn.

All that is left now is to clean the top with the cloth and leave 24 hours to set fully.


**NOTE:** if you are having difficulty removing the last of the silicone smear, use a small amount of white spirit on the cloth but not too much as it can wash out the silicone at the surface.

There are special tubes of matching colourant specially designed for applying to the top of the joint before assembly but if the joint is good and pulled up correctly, there is barely a crack for it to fill! and I rarely use it.

I tend to use a clear silicone or black silicone for black tops.

There are also special self-grip bolts available to help prevent the bolts dropping on the initial tightening up but I don't find it a problem and never use them.


DO NOT FIX DOWN THE WORKTOPS TO THE UNITS UNTIL AT LEAST 24 HOURS AFTER BOLTING UP TO GIVE THE SILICONE TIME TO CURE.

SCREWING THE TOPS DOWN CAN DEFLECT THEM AND CAUSE THE JOINT TO MOVE SO THAT IT IS NO LONGER FLUSH.

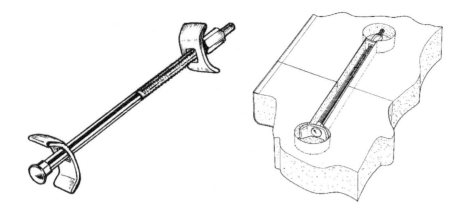

WORKTOP JOINTING BOLT          UNDERSIDE OF WOFKTOP SHOWING BOLT

## 8) FINISH OFF THE WORKTOP ENDS

The tops should have been supplied with a length of colour matched laminate edging strip which is glued to the ends using contact adhesive.

Snap off a length slightly longer than required. Usually this strip is slightly wider than the worktop thickness by about 3mm so unless you possess a laminate trimmer, just cut the surplus width off with a pair of stout scissors and the rounded end profile and place the good uncut edge uppermost.

When fixing the glued strip onto the chipboard, leave the front rounded edge slightly proud to allow for filing down flush. Take extreme care when filing down or you will file into the laminate surface of the worktop. (Gently does it)

# FIXING DOWN WORKTOPS

Simply screw up through the underside of the base unit front rails into the worktop, making sure that you clamp as you go to hold the surfaces together. Also reach into the unit and place a couple of screws at the back as well.

**NOTE:** if screwing into a solid oak top you will need a pilot hole or the screw may snap off.

# SEALING WORKTOP APERTURES

Before fitting the sink and hob the edges of the worktop apertures should be sealed with a PVA priming solution.

This is to prevent the possibility of chipboard worktops expanding in thickness in the event of water seeping through from the sink. (I also seal the hob aperture as well for good measure)

Use a mix of 50% PVA to 50% WATER applied with a small 1" paint brush.

# PLUMBING (Types of fittings)

I always use copper pipe for the plumbing (not plastic) In the past I was employed as an Installation manager for two major kitchen manufacturers and both companies insisted on copper due to customer complaints they had regarding plastic.

There are different types of fittings for use on copper pipe as follows:

**COMPRESSION** These are brass fittings with nuts that tighten up to compress a brass or copper olive which crimps onto the pipe to form the seal. (Expensive, time consuming and bulky in confined spaces) I use these fittings where soldering is out of the question, for instance when connecting onto a pipe which is dripping water from say a valve further up the line which will not fully turn off.

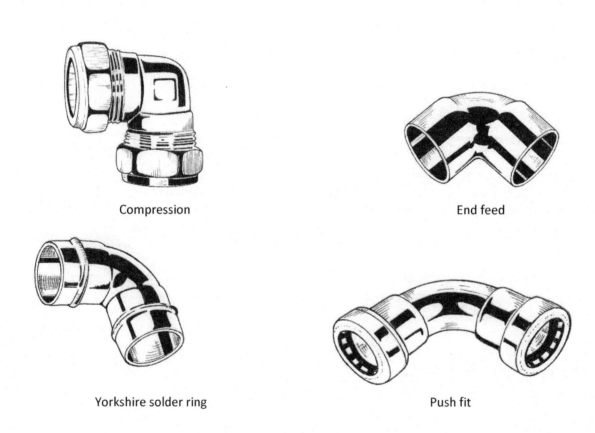

Compression

End feed

Yorkshire solder ring

Push fit

**YORKSHIRE SOLDER RING** These are copper fittings which have a ring of solidified solder at each end.

After cleaning the pipes with fine wire wool and applying flux the fitting is simply pushed onto both pipes and heated with a blow torch until the solder melts and is seen to emerge slightly from the joint.

(Expensive but convenient, especially in very tight spaces) Have coil of solder handy for topping up.

**END FEED**  These are my choice. Same as Yorkshire but you put the solder in.

After cleaning the pipes with fine wire wool and applying flux the fitting is pushed onto the pipes and heated with a blow torch.

As the fitting and the pipe heats up you will notice a discolouration taking place which will indicate that it is time to lightly touch the joint with the reel of plumbers solder. The solder will melt and run around the rim of the joint to make the seal (**DO NOT OVERHEAT** or the solder will vapourise off and not seal.)

Also remember **JUST A TOUCH** with the solder as you can fill up the fitting and reduce water flow or worse still the solder plug could break off inside.

Leave the joint to cool naturally for the first minute or so before wiping any residue flux off with a damp cloth which will also reduce the temperature of the pipe for handling.

Sounds complicated but believe me the majority of plumbers use these as they are relatively cheap if purchased in bulk bags and quick to use.

### REMEMBER TO USE LEAD FREE SOLDER FOR DRINKING WATER

**PUSH FIT COPPER FITTINGS.**  These are for speed but come at a high price!

Easy to use, just cut the end of the pipe nice and square with a pipe cutter and push home firmly.

(Very expensive and have the disadvantage of the pipework not being rigid due to the pipes being able to revolve in the fittings)

**PLASTIC PIPE FITTINGS.**  With the exception of the plastic push fit end stops (which are only used as a temporary measure) and metal braided hoses which have plastic push fit ends, I prefer not to use them in KITCHENS.

During a short spell of maintenance work when I came out of kitchens for a while, most of the plumbing faults I had to repair in domestic and commercial premises were related to plastic fittings.

## UNDERSINK PLUMBING (Final connections)

Fit the tap(s) to the sink and then fit the sink into the worktop. (It will be necessary to remove some of the base unit top rail to allow the sink to drop in)

With the sink clipped in as per the fitting instructions, it is now time to make the final connections up to the tap and also the dishwasher and washing machine if present.

The following diagram shows the finished job on a typical layout. (Obviously they all vary**)**

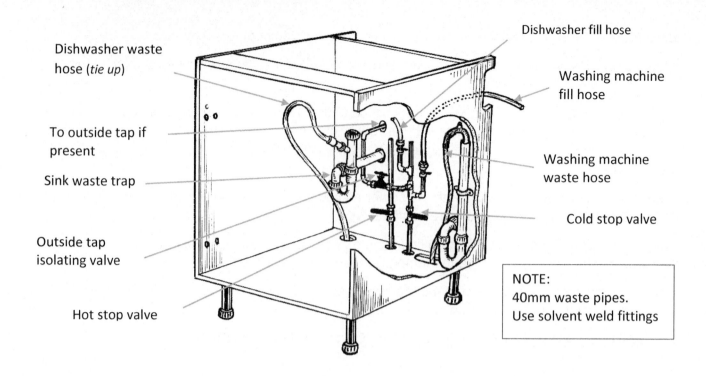

Dishwasher waste hose (*tie up*)

Dishwasher fill hose

Washing machine fill hose

To outside tap if present

Sink waste trap

Washing machine waste hose

Outside tap isolating valve

Cold stop valve

Hot stop valve

NOTE:
40mm waste pipes.
Use solvent weld fittings

**WARNING** - ALWAYS FLUSH OUT NEW PIPEWORK INTO A BUCKET BEFORE CONNECTING UP TO TAPS AND APPLIANCES TO REMOVE FLUX AND SWARF.

Flexible steel braided hoses with plastic push on connectors are my choice for running up to the taps.

If the sink trap is part of a "kit" supplied with the sink (especially if it is One and a half bowl) it will probably have two spigots on it for dishwasher and washing machine waste. I only use one of these which I connect to the dishwasher, preferring to fit a separate stand pipe waste for the washing machine to prevent soap suds from potentially come up through the sink plug hole. (Maybe I'm too fussy but I did have complaints of this in the early days)

The washing machine standpipe can be in an adjacent cupboard depending on the layout.

## CORNICE PELMETS AND PLINTHS

### CUTTING CORNICE AND PELMET (If present)

To cut the mitred angles you will need either a hand mitre saw or a powered mitre saw.

Powered is better and they range in price from cheap to very expensive.

With the powered option it is best to go for the pull out type as shown in the sketch with the extension bars clearly visible at the rear, these permit the saw to extend out to accommodate larger profiled sections and will also allow you to comfortably mitre 150mm width plinths as well.

The pull out ones are not cheap and the Hire shop is probably the best option.

Hand mitre saws again can be cheap or quite expensive.

As with all tools you get what you pay for.

A cheap hand mitre saw is rickety with a lot of play.

A cheap power saw lacks solid build quality, powerful long life motor and pull out facility.

**REMEMBER** if you are making a 45° angled corner cut each piece at 22.5°

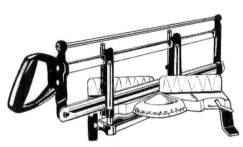

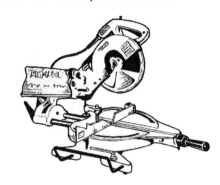

HAND MITRE SAW                                          POWERED MITRE SAW (Pull out Type)

## FIXING CORNICE TO WALL CABINETS

First remove all doors.

Drill pilot holes along the cornice first (To prevent splitting) and screw down from above.

If the wall units have little space above due to a low ceiling you will have to fix from below keeping the screws neat and even and all the same distance in from the edges of the cabinet for neatness. As mentioned before, avoid the specialist screws which have cutting ridges under the countersink for ease of penetration as they chip out the laminate.

I do not bother with countersinking, just go straight in with the screw using a cordless screwdriver and driving home until just below the surface.

## FIXING PELMET TO WALL CABINETS

You can either screw down through the cabinet directly into the pelmet below or use fixing blocks.

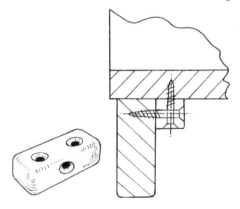

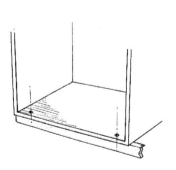

FIXING BLOCK                                                    DIRECT FIX

**<u>When fixing Pelmet be sure to clamp it in position before attempting to fix.</u>**

Strangely enough when screwing down through the cabinet not one single customer has ever complained at seeing the screws inside of the cupboard so this is the method I use (Keep it neat though)

I have had complaints with the block method though! The block method does not pull the pelmet up as tight and if you have under pelmet lights they can shine through the thin gap between the pelmet and cabinet.

This can be cured by running a bead of dark silicone along the rear of the pelmet but why bother with all this if nobody complains and the other method looks fine and takes a third of the time!

**TOP TIP** When fitting the pelmet returns back to the wall cut them short of the wall to allow for a wall tile to slide under with adhesive. (Much easier than trying to cut a tile around a profiled section of pelmet.)

### GLUING THE JOINTS

The best adhesive to date (It has changed over the years) is the two part superglue which is made specifically for the purpose.

It consists of the glue which is squeezed onto one half of the joint and a spray which is sprayed onto the other half. The parts are then brought together and held for 15 seconds to produce a very strong bond.

The adhesive is designed for use on MDF and chipboard but it also works well on pine. Oak sticks adequately enough but will knock apart fairly easily. (However when fixed to the cabinet it is fine)

**WARNING** Do not get this product on your fingers. I was once stranded with my arm above my head, stuck to a piece of high level cornice. Cutting my finger away with a "Stanley" knife blade is something I will never forget to this day!

**TOP TIP** Wall units can look much nicer if an end panel is fixed to each end of the run and the pelmet fixed between them instead of returning at the ends. This does cost more due to the high cost of end panels and you must also follow this through down below with the base unit plinths set between end panels to keep the alinement going.

Although I often set the PELMET between end panels I always finish the end panel flush with the top of the unit and return the CORNICE in the normal way.

44

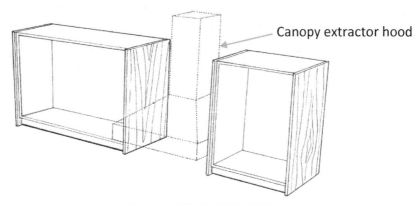

Canopy extractor hood

## WALL CABINETS WITH END PANELS AND CAPTIVE PELMET

### OVERHANG OF CORNICE – COMMON MISTAKE

Below is a sketch of how the cornice should overhang the end of the wall unit.

You should imagine that the end of the wall unit is a door and then overhang the cornice the same as the front. The diagram below should make this clear.

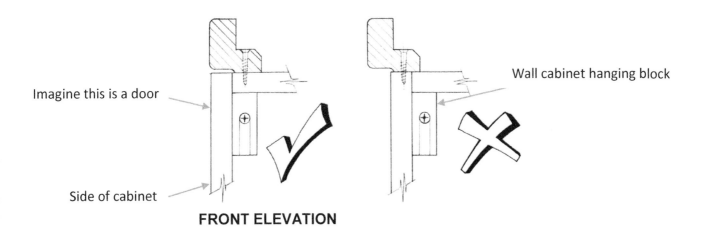

Imagine this is a door

Wall cabinet hanging block

Side of cabinet

**FRONT ELEVATION**

### CUTTING AND FIXING PLINTHS

The plinths are normally 150mm high but do vary.

When cutting an external corner there are two ways of finishing off the exposed ends.

You could just cut the ends square and glue on a piece of matching laminate tape (Often this is the iron on type) or you could mitre the ends and glue them together using the two part super glue.

**REMEMBER** if you are making a 45° angled corner you need to set the cut angle at 22.5° on each piece.

If you do decide to mitre them it is best to use the "pull out" type of powered mitre saw which usually means the Hire Shop. The Pull Out facility allows the machine to cut the large depth of 150mm.

The plinths are removable and held on by plastic or metal leg clips and for this reason they should not be a tight fit between the floor and the underside of the cabinet

I often run the entire length of the plinth through a table saw and remove 3mm off the top edge to allow for easy fitting and removal, when fitted you cannot see the rough cut top edge.

Where an integrated dishwasher is fitted the plinth will require notching out on the top edge to allow the door to swing down into the plinth when lowered. (Seal notch with PVA sealer)

# TILING TOOLS

MANUAL TILE CUTTER

ELECTRIC TILE CUTTER

TILE SNIPS

ADHESIVE NOTCHED TROWEL

GROUTING RUBBER BACKED TROWEL

SET SQUARE

The **MANUAL TILE CUTTER** is used for scoring and snapping tiles to width and also for scoring both lines on an L shaped piece.

For cutting floor tiles and some of the thicker wall tiles a decent robust cutter is required.

Without mentioning any names, the best in my opinion is made in Spain and is a "gem"! not cheap though.

**ELECTRIC TILE CUTTERS** have a diamond coated circular blade which dips into a water bath underneath to keep dust down and prolong blade life.

## CUTTING L SHAPED TILES (AROUND ELECTRICAL SOCKETS ETC)

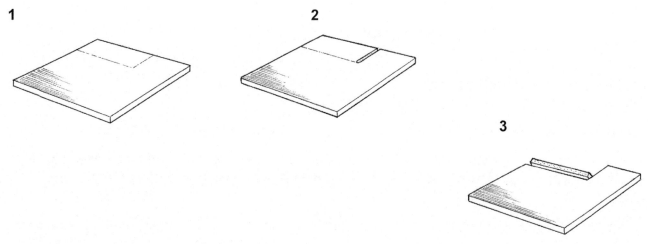

**1**          **2**

                                                          **3**

**1 SCORE      2 CUT      3 SNAP**

After both lines have been scored, I usually cut the short line with the diamond blade electric tile cutter followed by the manual tile cutter which snaps off the waste piece. However if the longest part of the L happens to be very narrow and likely to break on snapping I will sometimes cut both lines with the electric tiling machine as the very act of snapping can ruin the tile.

Snapping off a scored line from a manual tiling machine will produce a cleaner chip free finish.

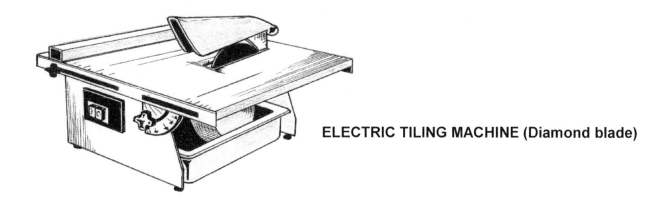

**ELECTRIC TILING MACHINE (Diamond blade)**

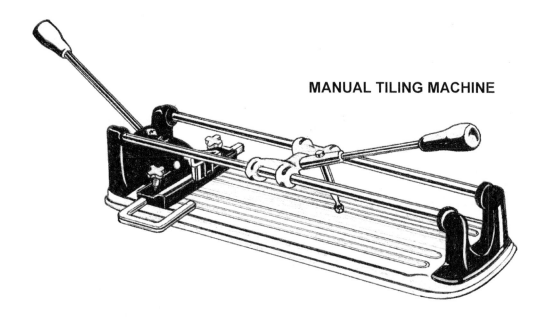

**MANUAL TILING MACHINE**

# TILING ABOVE WORKTOPS

Work out the exact area and add on 10% for wastage (cuts)

Give the wall a brush over with PVA / water primer and allow to become sticky before commencing tiling.

Always use tile spacers, never butt directly together.

### TILE ADHESIVE

I use the large ready mixed tubs (Avoid combined grout and adhesive)

### TILE TRIMS

These are used to finish off the tile edges and are available to suit different tile thicknesses.

NOTE: If using thick rustic tiles in an old country style cottage I dispense with the trims prefering to make a 45° chamfer on the grout edge.

**TOP TIP** Jack up the first level of tiles by laying tile spacers flat onto the worktop surface as shown below. This provides a gap for the silicone to enter when you finally seal the tops after tiling.

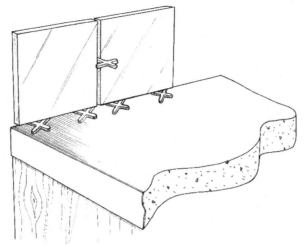

## WHERE TO START

As the cooker and hob are the centre feature of the kitchen I like the tiles to be centrally positioned at this point.

Start by drawing a vertical line dead centre of the hob and project it up to the cooker hood.

Now you need to determine whether it is better to place the tiles on the centre line or either side of the line. This will depend on your tile size (don't forget to allow for the spacers)

When you have made your decision double check by positioning the rest of tiles along the entire length of the top to see exactly how the ends finish up as you don't want to end up with a thin tile sliver that looks awful.

After looking at the complete picture again and if you are still happy you can commence tiling at the hob position and work out from either side.

When tiling bathrooms I tend to apply adhesive to a large wall area and then place the tiles into position.

However with a kitchen with its sockets and low wall units, it can be difficult to get a good sweep of the notched trowel and for this reason I tend to apply the adhesive to the tiles themselves when tiling around any obstructions.

**REMEMBER** tiles are cut around the socket boxes, not the surface plates. The plate then overlaps the edges of the tiles when fitted.

Just as I centre the tiles on the hob I also the centre tiles on the window to ensure the same width of tile each side of the window. Again mark the centre line and make a decision as to whether you start with a tile on the centre line or either side.


## GROUT AND SILICONE   (Allow 24hrs before grouting.)

Best type of grout applicator is the rubber backed trowel.
 I personally only use the powdered variety of grout that you mix with water.
Always use genuine silicone not a cheap alternative.

**TOP TIP** Avoid combined grout and adhesive as the adhesive is not so good and the grout dries hard and is difficult to finish.

## GROUTING

Before commencing go around the whole tiled area with a flat scraper to remove any surface adhesive lumps and a small screwdriver to prise out any tile spacers which are standing proud.

Grout a small area at a time (approx. 1m sq) using a rubber backed grouting trowel.

Use the same trowel to remove the surplus grout on the surface and also between the joints. As you move around the room you will notice the previously applied grout starts to powder over, this is the time to rub over the tiles using a dry cloth (old pillow case ideal)

As my hands are hard from years of fitting, I run my fingers along the grout lines to finish off the joints but it is not recommended. Use either the corner of the rubber grouting trowel or place a piece of thin cloth over the end of your finger.

## SILICONE

First of all remove the "flat" tile spacers that were used to jack up the tiles. Then using a thin scrapper remove any grout from within the gap under the tiles.

Run a vacuum around the gap to remove all traces of grout and then wipe any traces of dust from the worktop for about 50mm in front of the tiles to allow good adhesion for the masking tape.

**TOP TIP** Position masking tape along the whole length of the section to have silicone applied.

The tape is applied to both the tiles and the worktop with a gap of approximately 5mm between the two tapes. (The gap should look in proportion to the thickness of tile spacer used)

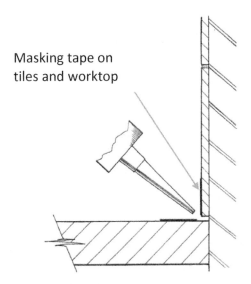

Masking tape on tiles and worktop

**TAPING JOINT FOR SILICONE**

Using the silicone gun, run a bead of silicone along the entire length.

Without waiting for the silicone to skin over, immediately run your finger along the bead and press it firmly into the gap. (If the gap is deep another bead may be necessary on top which is again pressed in firmly as your finger moves along)

Now immediately peel off the two strips of tape leaving a clean straight bead.

If you prefer a softer look to the bead, wet your finger and lightly run it along the entire length immediately after removing the tape.

# THE END

## FUTURE PUBLICATIONS

**A TILERS GUIDE TO KITCHENS AND BATHROOMS  By *Joe Luker***

**HOW TO PLAN A KITCHEN  By *Joe Luker***

**HOW TO BUILD CUSTOM PLASTERBOARD ARCHES *By Joe Luker***

## ABOUT THE AUTHOR

Joe Luker was born in Slough in 1952 the son of a skilled carpenter. At school he excelled at Woodwork and Technical Drawing, then started his working career as a Trainee Draughtsman with Parker Knoll Furniture Ltd in High Wycombe, the furniture capital of England.

Over the next 10 years while still working full time he gained professional qualifications in both Furniture Craft and Mechanical Engineering and attained the position of Senior Design Draughtsman with Beecham Proprietaries in Maidenhead.

However, his true love was working with tools so in 1983 he decide to become self-employed designing and fitting kitchens - a career he has continued for over 30 years.

## ALL ILLUSTRATIONS BY THE AUTHOR.

### ACKNOWLEDGEMENTS
This book is dedicated to my long suffering wife Lesley who has endured many house renovations and without whose assistance this book would not have been possible.

Printed in Great Britain
by Amazon

37113681R00031